The Stars

by Martha E. H. Rustad

Consulting Editor: Gail Saunders-Smith, Ph.D.
Consultant: James Gerard
Aerospace Education Specialist
Kennedy Space Center

Pebble Books

an imprint of Capstone Press
Mankato, Minnesota

Pebble Books are published by Capstone Press
151 Good Counsel Drive, P.O. Box 669, Mankato, Minnesota 56002
http://www.capstone-press.com

1 2 3 4 5 6 07 06 05 04 03 02

Library of Congress Cataloging-in-Publication Data
Rustad, Martha E. H. (Martha Elizabeth Hillman), 1975–
    The stars / by Martha E. H. Rustad.
    p. cm.—(Out in space)
    Includes bibliographical references and index.
    Summary: An easy-to-read introduction to stars and their characteristics.
ISBN 0-7368-1179-6
1. Stars—Juvenile literature. [1. Stars.] I. Title. II. Series.
QB801.7 .R87 2002
523.8—dc21   2001004838

Note to Parents and Teachers

The Out in Space series supports national science standards for
units on the universe. This book describes and illustrates the
stars. The photographs support early readers in understanding
the text. This book also introduces early readers to subject-specific
vocabulary words, which are defined in the Words to Know section.
Early readers may need assistance to read some words and to use
the Table of Contents, Words to Know, Read More, Internet Sites,
and Index/Word List sections of the book.

Table of Contents

What Is a Star? 5

The Life of Stars. 15

The Sun 21

Words to Know 22

Read More 23

Internet Sites 23

Index/Word List. 24

Look up in the night sky.
The stars twinkle and shine.

6

From Earth, stars look like small lights. Some stars are bright.
Some stars are dim.

8

A star is a huge ball
of gases out in space.
The gases burn and
give off light and heat.

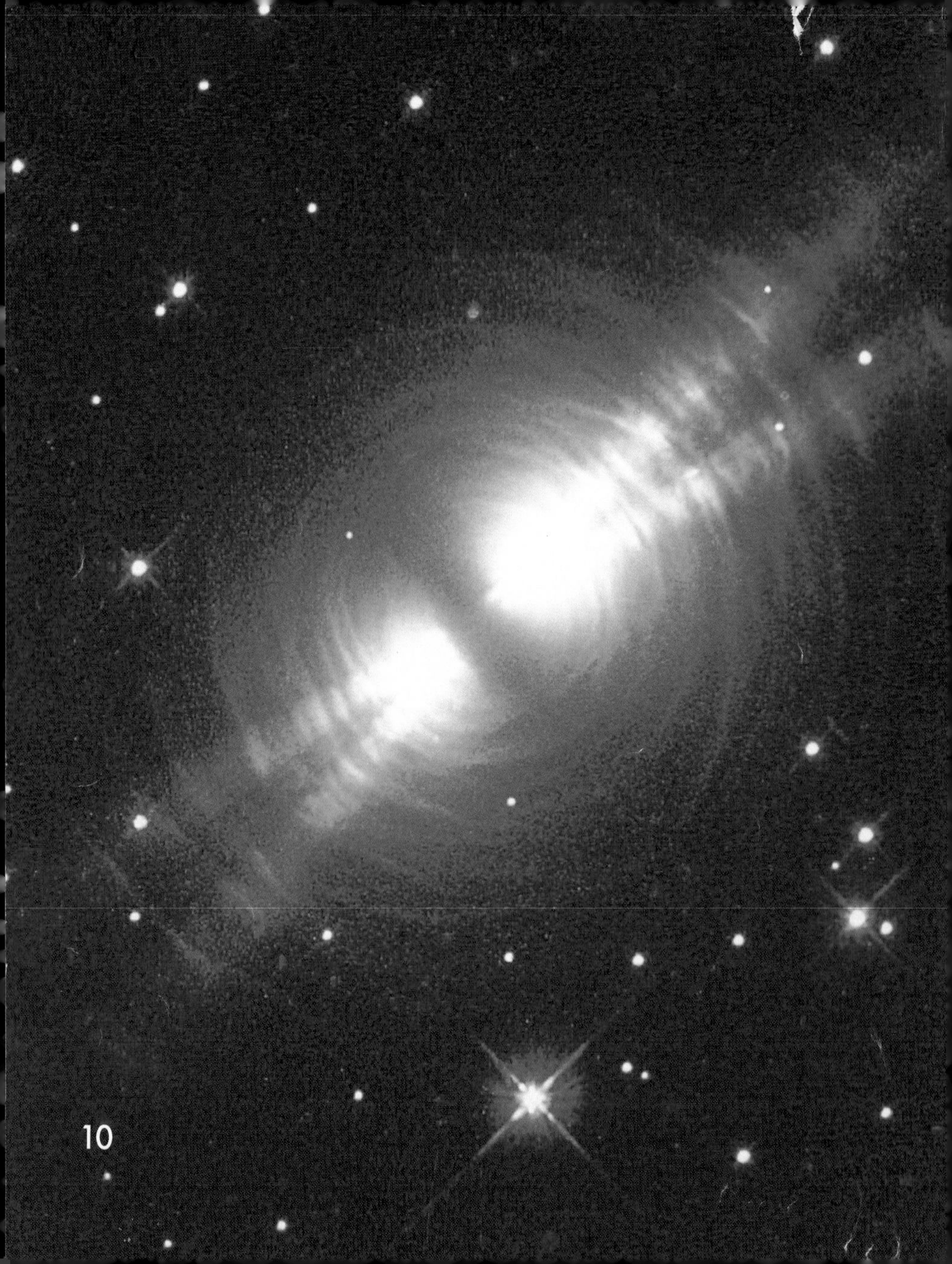

Some stars group together
in clusters.

yellow star

white star

orange star

blue star
hottest kind of star

red star
coldest kind of star

Stars are different colors and different temperatures.

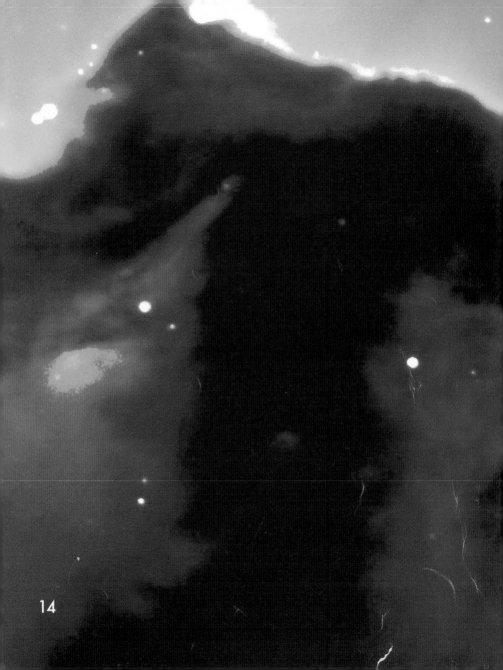

Dust and gases
in space come together
to make stars.

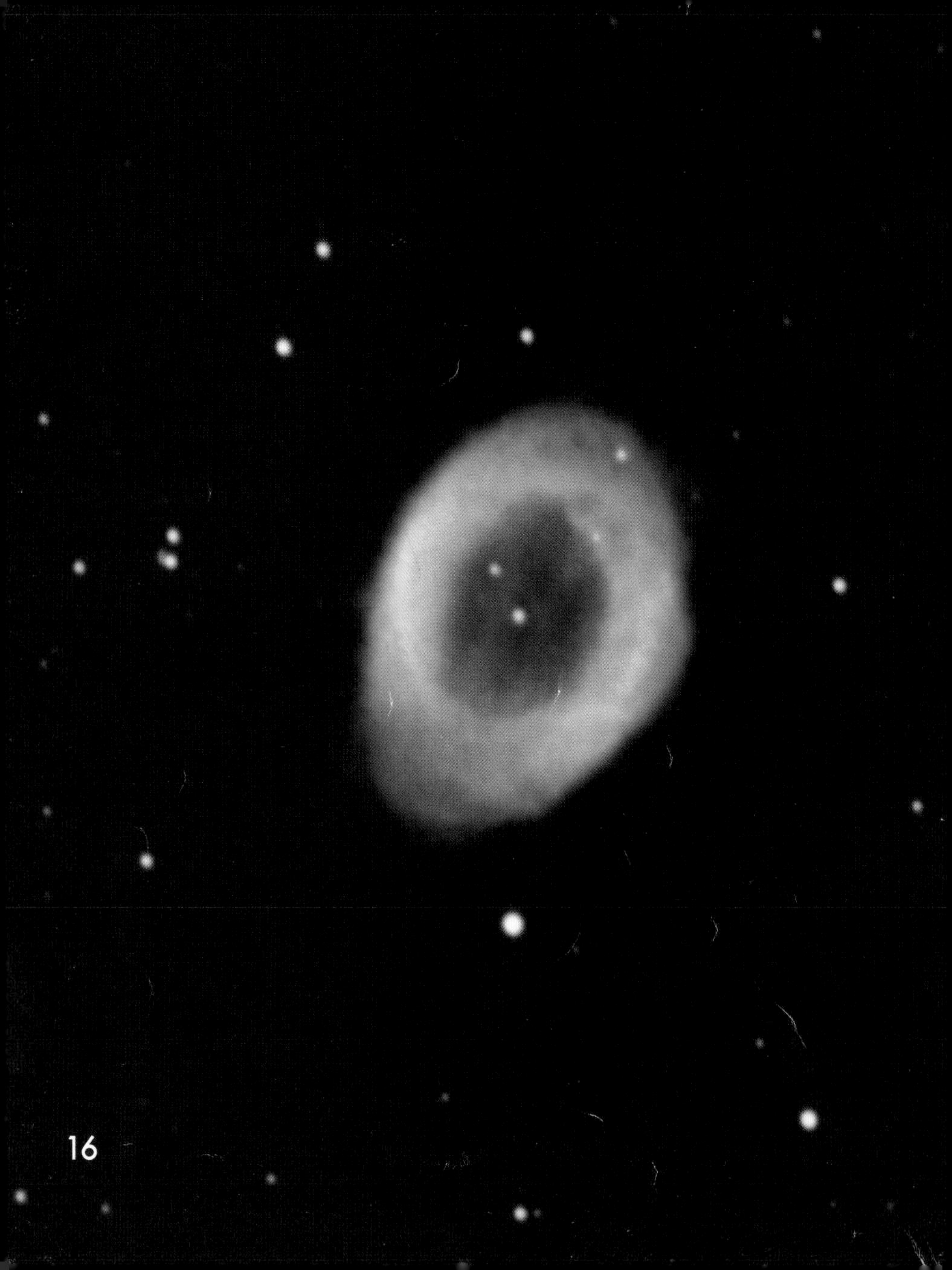

Stars grow larger
as they grow older.
Some stars explode
when they die.

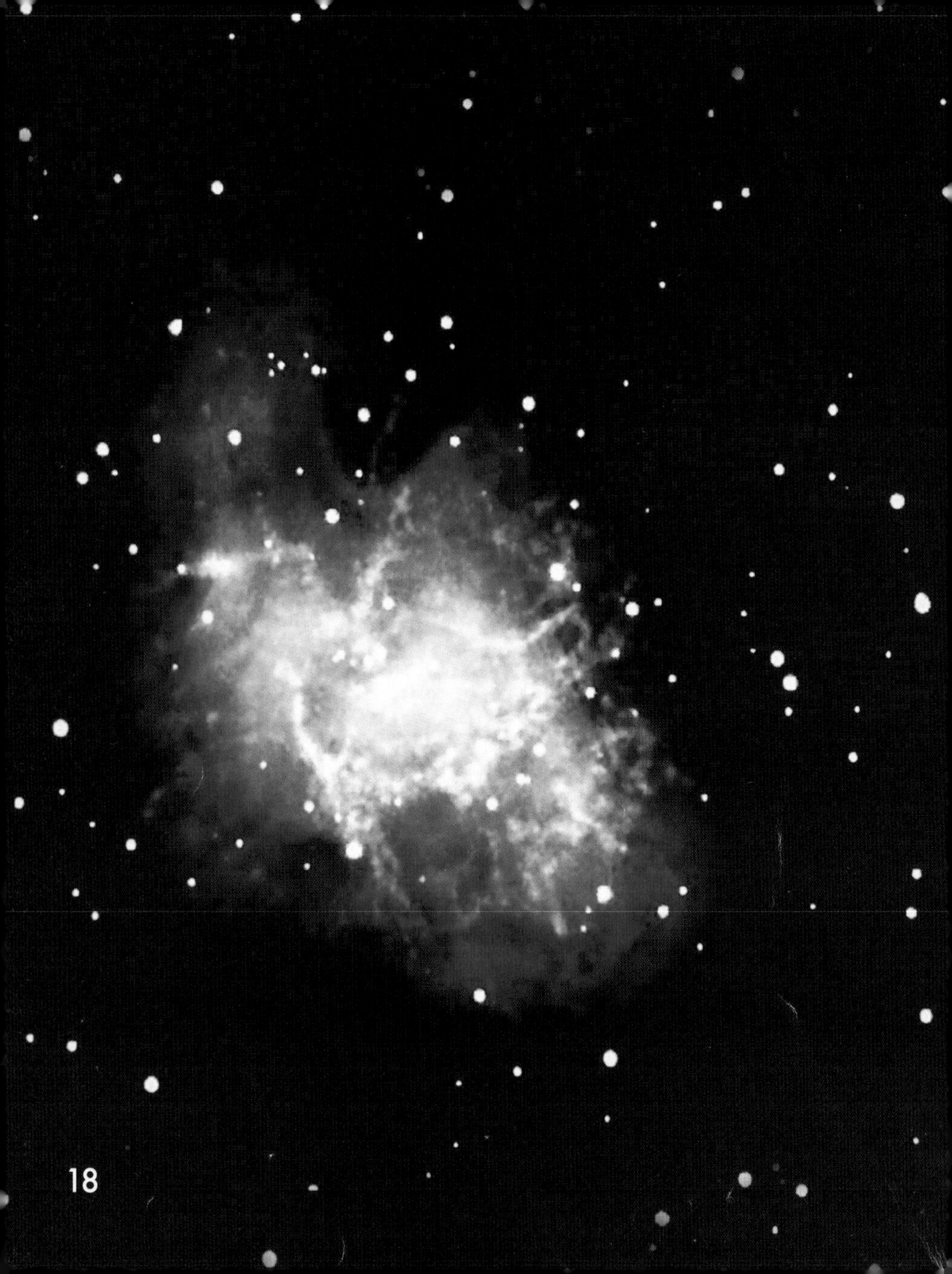

Most stars live for billions of years.

The sun is a yellow star.
It is the closest star
to Earth.

Words to Know

cluster—a group of objects that are close together; a star cluster can contain thousands of stars.

dim—not very bright

Earth—the planet where we live; Earth is about 93 million miles (150 million kilometers) from the sun, its closest star.

explode—to blow apart with great force

gas—a substance that spreads to fill any space that holds it

temperature—the measure of how hot or cold something is

twinkle—to shine or sparkle

yellow star—a medium-sized star; the sun is a yellow star; the temperature of the sun is about 10,500 degrees Fahrenheit (5,800 degrees Celsius).

Read More

Cobb, Allan B. *How Do We Know How Stars Shine?* Great Scientific Questions and the Scientists Who Answered Them. New York: Rosen, 2001.

Marzollo, Jean. *I Am a Star.* Hello Science Reader! New York: Scholastic, 2000.

Vogt, Gregory L. *Stars.* The Galaxy. Mankato, Minn.: Bridgestone Books, 2002.

Internet Sites

BrainPOP: Life Cycle of Stars
http://www.brainpop.com/science/space/starscycle

Constellations
http://www.fcps.k12.va.us/DIS/OHSICS/
planet/constell/constell.htm

Sky Watch
http://school.discovery.com/schooladventures/skywatch

StarChild: A Learning Center for Young Astronomers
http://starchild.gsfc.nasa.gov/docs/StarChild

Index/Word List

ball, 9
billions, 19
bright, 7
burn, 9
closest, 21
clusters, 11
colors, 13
die, 17
dim, 7
dust, 15

Earth, 7, 21
explode, 17
gases, 9, 15
grow, 17
heat, 9
light, 7, 9
night, 5
older, 17
shine, 5
sky, 5

small, 7
space, 9, 15
sun, 21
temperatures, 13
together, 11, 15
twinkle, 5
years, 19
yellow, 21

Word Count: 102
Early-Intervention Level: 15

Credits
Timothy Halldin, cover designer and interior illustrator; Kimberly Danger, Mary Englar, and Jo Miller, photo researchers

Bill & Sally Fletcher/TOM STACK & ASSOCIATES, 4
Bill Schoening/NOAO/AURA/NSF, 16
NASA, 20
PhotoDisc, Inc., cover, 1, 6, 8, 10, 12, 14, 18